CW00522396

Pompeii Travel Guide 2024

"Sunrise To Sunset: A Day In Pompeii, Italy"

James Frazer

Copyright © 2024 James Frazer.
All rights reserved.
No part of this publication may be
reproduced, distributed, or transmitted in
any form or by any means, including
photocopying, recording, or other
electronic or mechanical methods,
without the prior written permission of
the publisher, except in the case of brief
quotations embodied in critical reviews
and certain other noncommercial uses
permitted by copyright

GAIN ACCESS TO MORE BOOKS FROM ME

TABLE OF CONTENTS

Chapter 1

Introduction To Pompeii

Pompeii is a historic city in Italy that was trapped in time by Mount Vesuvius' devastating eruption in 79 AD. It is situated close to Naples today. This chapter introduces Pompeii, giving background information and a summary of the reasons why it is still a popular tourism destination in 2024.

1.1 Background and Synopsis

Around the sixth century BC, an Italic tribe known as the Oscans established Pompeii. Later, in the first century BC, it was established as a Roman colony and flourished as a thriving port city and a popular vacation spot for affluent Romans.

When Mount Vesuvius erupted on August 24, 79 AD, burying Pompeii behind a thick layer of volcanic ash and pumice, the city's destiny was drastically altered. Because of this terrible incident, Pompeii was unusually well preserved, giving scholars a rare glimpse into Roman culture.

Pompeii's extraordinarily well-preserved structures, streets, and artifacts provide unmatched insights into everyday life in ancient Rome. Excavations of the site started in the 18th century. One of the most visited archeological sites worldwide, Pompeii is recognized as a UNESCO World Heritage Site today.

1.2 Why Go to Pompeii in the Year 2024?

In 2024, there will be a rare chance to see one of the most important archeological sites on Earth when you visit Pompeii. Pompeii is still a popular tourist destination for the following reasons:

1) **Historical Significance:** Pompeii offers a unique window into everyday life in ancient Rome, shedding light on the period's social systems, architecture, art, and culture.

2) **Amazing Preservation:** Pompeii's buildings, frescoes, and antiques have been conserved to an unmatched degree, enabling tourists to stroll through historic streets and discover immaculately maintained homes, apartments, and public areas.

3) Discoveries are constantly being made during ongoing excavations and study, which illuminates various facets of Pompeii's past and makes every visit to the site distinct and enlightening.

4) **Educational Value:** Through guided tours, interactive displays, and educational programs, Pompeii gives visitors of all ages educational

opportunities that provide insights into archeology, geology, history, and ancient Roman society.

5) Pompeii provides a cultural experience in addition to its historical relevance because of its proximity to Naples, a city known for its mouthwatering cuisine, lively street life, and rich cultural legacy.

6) **Sustainable Tourism:** To guarantee that future generations may continue to enjoy and learn from this amazing place, efforts are being made to encourage sustainable tourism and protect the delicate archaeological remains of Pompeii.

Travelers may establish a connection with history, learn more about ancient civilizations, and recognize the need to conserve cultural legacy for future generations by visiting Pompeii in 2024.

Chapter 2

Making Travel Plans

When organizing a trip to Pompeii, it's important to take into account several variables, such as the ideal time to go, available lodging, and modes of transportation. This chapter offers comprehensive information to assist travelers in making well-informed travel plans.

2.1 When Is the Best Time to Go?

When the weather is moderate and there are fewer tourists than during the busiest summer months, spring (April to June) and fall (September to October) are the ideal times to visit Pompeii.

Visitors may peacefully tour the ancient site during these months, away from the oppressive heat and big crowds.

1)The summer, which runs from July to August, is Pompeii's busiest travel season because of the warmer weather and more tourists.

Even though it might become hot and muggy at this time of year, tourists can still have a great time if they arrive early in the morning or late in the afternoon to escape the heat and congestion around lunchtime.

2)The low visitor season in Pompeii is winter, which runs from November to March and is marked by chilly weather and sporadic showers.

Even though fewer people arrive during this period, some services and attractions can have shortened hours or be closed.

Winter tourists, on the other hand, will find Pompeii to be more peaceful and personal, with fewer people to deal with.

The ideal time to visit Pompeii ultimately relies on personal choices, since each season offers different benefits and experiences.

2.2 Transportation to Pompeii

By Train:

1) By rail from Naples or Sorrento to Pompeii is the most convenient option.

2) Travel from Naples to Sorrento on the Circumvesuviana rail line, then get down at the Pompeii Scavi-Villa dei Misteri station, which is a short walk from the archeological site's entrance.

3) Travel from Sorrento to Naples by rail on the Circumvesuviana line, getting out at the Pompeii Scavi-Villa dei Misteri station.

Via Automobile:

1) Pompeii is also accessible by automobile, and there are many parking lots close to the archeological site.

2) Depending on your direction of travel, get out of either Pompeii Ovest or Pompeii Est off the A3 highway (Autostrada Napoli-Salerno) near Naples.

3) To get to Pompeii, use the SS145 highway and follow the signs from Sorrento or the Amalfi Coast.

2.3 Places to Stay

Pompeii has a variety of lodging choices, including hotels, bed & breakfasts, holiday rentals, and campsites, to accommodate a range of tastes and price ranges. Here are a few well-liked places to stay in and near Pompeii:

1)Hotels: There are several hotels in the vicinity of the Pompeii archeological site, ranging in price from luxurious lodging to more affordable choices. Modern conveniences like Wi-Fi, air conditioning, and on-site dining are available at many hotels.

2)Bed & Breakfasts: For those looking for a more individualized and private experience, bed and breakfasts are a popular option. Numerous bed & breakfasts in Pompeii provide comfortable lodging and freshly prepared meals in quaint antique houses.

3)Vacation Rentals: For those looking for more room and seclusion, there are vacation rentals—including apartments and villas—available in and around Pompeii. Families and groups of friends will find vacation rentals suitable since they frequently include kitchens and other amenities.

4)Campsites: Near Pompeii, some campgrounds provide RV and tent camping for outdoor lovers. Campsites around the archeological site provide minimal services including showers, toilets, and laundry rooms, enabling visitors to have a relaxed and rustic camping experience.

It is recommended that visitors reserve their housing in advance to guarantee a pleasant stay at Pompeii, particularly during the busiest travel season.

Chapter 3

Pompeii Exploration

Discovering Pompeii is an amazing trip through a historic Roman city brought to a standstill by Mount Vesuvius' explosion in 79 AD. This chapter offers comprehensive details on the main attractions of the archaeological site, explains the advantages of guided tours over self-guided excursions, and includes a map of the Pompeii Archaeological Site to aid tourists in efficiently navigating the area.

3.1 Principal Attractions

Many well-preserved structures, relics, and monuments that provide light on everyday life in ancient Rome may be found in Pompeii. Among the most popular sights at the archeological site are:

1) **Pompeii Forum:** The Forum served as the city's principal public space and municipal hub and was considered the heart of ancient Pompeii. The Comitium, the Basilica, and the Temple of Jupiter are among the highlights.

2) **House of the Faun:** Known for its intricate mosaic flooring, which includes the renowned Alexander Mosaic that portrays the Battle of Issus, the House of the Faun is one of Pompeii's most opulent homes.

3) The exquisite murals of the Villa of the Mysteries, which is well-preserved, are well-known. Among them is the mysterious "Dionysian Mysteries" fresco cycle, which shows scenes from initiation procedures.

4) **Pompeii Amphitheater:** This magnificent building, which is among

the oldest Roman amphitheaters still standing, was once the site of gladiatorial matches and other events.

5) Plaster casts of those who died in the eruption may be seen in the heartbreaking Garden of the Fugitives, offering a somber window into the human tragedy of Pompeii's devastation.

6) The Street of Abundance, one of Pompeii's principal thoroughfares, is flanked by stores, bars, and historic storefronts that provide an insight into the city's everyday commerce.

These are only a few of the many attractions that the Pompeii archeological site has to offer, each providing a different perspective on the history and culture of the ancient city.

3.2 Tours that are Guided vs. Self-Guided

Visitors may choose to go on self-guided tours or join guided tours conducted by experienced tour operators to see Pompeii on their own. Here are some things to think about for each choice:

1)Guided Tours: Guided tours provide guests with a comprehensive understanding of the history, architecture, and way of life of Pompeii.

Experienced guides improve the visiting experience by providing context and explanation. For those who want to get a thorough grasp of Pompeii's importance and features, guided excursions are highly recommended.

2)Self-Guided Tours: Using pre-marked paths and focusing on areas of particular interest, self-guided tours let tourists explore Pompeii at their speed.

To explore the site on their own, visitors may make use of smartphone applications, audio tours, or guidebooks. Self-guided excursions provide guests with flexibility and autonomy, enabling them to explore off-the-beaten-path locations and spend more time at their favorite sights.

Visitors to Pompeii are certain to be enthralled by the archeological treasures that lie behind the walls of the ancient city, whether they choose a guided or self-guided tour.

3.3 Map of the Pompeii Archaeological Site

To navigate the vast remains of the Pompeii archeological site safely, a thorough map is a must. Key features, walkways, bathrooms, and other amenities are usually highlighted on the map.

Before visiting Pompeii, visitors may download digital maps from the official websites or mobile applications, or they can pick one up at the entry.

The Pompeii Archaeological Site Map facilitates tourists' navigation, allows them to rank the sites in order of importance, and guarantees a seamless and pleasurable discovery of this amazing ancient city.

Chapter 4

Pompeii's Must-See Locations

Numerous archeological riches, including well-preserved structures, public areas, and works of art, may be found at Pompeii. The Pompeii Forum and the House of the Faun are two must-see locations within the Pompeii archeological site that are highlighted in this chapter.

4.1 Forum Pompeii

The political, economic, and religious hub of the ancient city was the Pompeii Forum, also known as the Forum of Pompeii. This large public plaza served as the center of everyday activity in Pompeii and was encircled by significant municipal structures and temples.

Important characteristics:

1) **Temple of Jupiter:** The principal temple devoted to the most important god in the Roman pantheon, the Temple of Jupiter (Tempio di Giove) dominated the northern side of the Forum. Ancient Roman architecture is reflected in the grandeur of its towering remnants.

2) **Basilica:** The Basilica is a large public structure next to the Temple of Jupiter that serves as a courtroom and administrative hub. It functioned as a gathering spot for business meetings and court cases, with colonnades around the central nave.

3) **Comitium:** Also known as the Curia, the Comitium served as the meeting place for local magistrates and municipal authorities to conduct public business and debate civic issues.

4) **Caligula's Arch:** Also called the Arch of Tiberius, this imposing arch honored Emperor Caligula's 37 AD visit to Pompeii and marked the entry to the Forum from the Via dell'Abbondanza.

Explore the remnants of these important buildings in the Pompeii Forum to learn more about the social, political, and religious life of ancient Pompeii.

4.2 House Of The Faun

One of the biggest and most opulent homes in Pompeii is called the House of the Faun (Casa del Fauno), after a bronze statue of a dancing faun that was discovered there. This opulent mansion is well known for its stunning mosaic flooring, ornate décor, and striking architecture.

Important characteristics:

1) **Atrium:** The House of the Faun's central atrium is home to a large impluvium, or submerged water basin, that is encircled by columns and embellished with sculptures and other ornamental pieces.

2) **Alexander Mosaic:** One of the most well-known mosaics in Pompeii, the Alexander Mosaic shows King Darius III of Persia and Alexander the Great engaged in the Battle of Issus. A masterwork of ancient Roman craftsmanship, this elaborate mosaic covers the floor of the exedra (welcome chamber).

3) **Peristyle Garden:** The villa's peristyle garden has rich landscaping, a central fountain, and is encircled by columns. It functioned as a personal outdoor area for leisure and entertainment.

4) **Tablinum:** The House of the Faun's study, or tablinum, was used as a guest reception hall and was decorated with murals that portrayed scenes from mythology.

The House of the Faun displays the artistic and architectural triumphs of ancient Rome while providing a window into the lavish lifestyle of Pompeii's aristocratic citizens.

Visitors get a greater understanding of Pompeii's rich history and cultural legacy by seeing these must-see locations in the ancient Roman city.

4.3 The Mysterious Villa

One of Pompeii's most fascinating and well-preserved villas is the Villa of the Mysteries (Villa dei Misteri), which is well-known for its breathtaking murals that portray events from the Dionysian Mysteries, a covert religious cult honoring the deity Dionysus. Visitors may get a unique insight into the spiritual and religious rituals of ancient Pompeii by staying at this home.

Important characteristics:

1) The most notable feature of the Villa of the Mysteries is the amazing murals that cover the walls of many rooms. The most well-known fresco cycle features several intriguing and mysterious scenarios about the Dionysian Mysteries initiation ceremonies. These striking and moving murals provide light on the customs, symbols, and beliefs of this archaic religion.

2) **Triclinium:** The villa's dining room, or triclinium, is decorated with murals that show a variety of banqueting and entertainment scenarios. The triclinium's design and

embellishments imply that it was used to hold opulent feasts and social events.

3) **Courtyard & Gardens:** The Villa of the Mysteries is encircled by beautifully designed courtyards and gardens, offering a serene environment for unwinding and reflection. The outside areas of the villa are designed with lush vegetation, ornamental fountains, and architectural features that blend in with the overall site aesthetic.

4) **Architecture:** With well-appointed apartments, exquisite courtyards, and complex architectural features, the Villa of the Mysteries' architecture reflects the opulent lifestyle of its owners. The arrangement and style of the villa highlight the creativity and skill of classical Roman buildings.

With its amazing paintings and stunning architecture, a visit to the Villa of the Mysteries provides a fascinating look into the religion, art, and culture of ancient Rome.

4.4 Pompeii's Amphitheater

One of the earliest Roman amphitheaters still standing, the Pompeii Amphitheater offers evidence of the lively entertainment scene in the city. The people of ancient Pompeii were amused by gladiatorial matches, animal hunts, and other events held in this magnificent building.

Important characteristics:

1) **Architecture:** With its elliptical form, tiered seating, and arena floor, the Pompeii Amphitheater is a perfect example of Roman amphitheater architecture. Built of brick and volcanic tuff, the structure's well-preserved remnants demonstrate

the Roman architects' mastery of engineering.

2) **Seating:** Up to 20,000 people may be seated in the amphitheater to observe a range of activities, including theatrical productions, gladiatorial competitions, and wild animal hunts. The lowest tiers nearest to the arena accommodated the most affluent spectators, while the upper tiers offered seats at varying degrees of social standing.

3) **Arena:** The Pompeii Amphitheater's arena floor served as the main stage for all of the events that took place there. It had trapdoors for dramatic effects and unexpected entrances, as well as devices for raising and lowering actors and animals.

4) **Historical Significance:** As one of the oldest Roman amphitheaters still standing and a representation of the

vibrant cultural legacy of the city, the Pompeii Amphitheater is significant historically. Its well-preserved ruins provide insightful information about the social dynamics and entertainment customs of classical Pompeii.

A trip to Pompeii's Amphitheater offers a window into the thriving entertainment scene of ancient Rome by allowing tourists to go back in time and picture the exciting shows that once took place within.

Chapter 5

Pompeii Travel Tips

Careful preparation is necessary to guarantee a successful and pleasurable trip to Pompeii. This chapter offers vital travel advice on packing for the trip, safety precautions to take, and suggested restaurants and shops in Pompeii.

5.1 Things to Bring

It's crucial to pack sensibly for your trip to Pompeii to guarantee comfort and convenience while seeing the ancient site. The following are some necessities to think about before packing:

1) Proper footwear is necessary for touring Pompeii's ruins comfortably due to its uneven terrain and size as a major archeological site. Select robust, well-traction shoes with closed

toes to safely negotiate the historic streets and walkways.

2) Pompeii is known for its bright and exposed weather, so while visiting the site, be sure to bring sun protection items like sunscreen, sunglasses, and a wide-brimmed hat to protect yourself from the sun's rays.

3) **Water and Snacks:** Bring a reusable water bottle to stay hydrated throughout your visit. Pack some fruit or energy bars as well so you have something to eat while seeing Pompeii.

4) **Weather-appropriate Clothes:** Before your vacation, check the forecast and pack appropriately. Layers are advised for colder months or bad weather, while lightweight, breathable clothing is advised for hot summer days.

5) **Backpack or Daypack:** Bring a compact backpack or daypack to hold your necessities, such as water, food, sunscreen, and any mementos or purchases you make while there.

6) Bring a camera or smartphone with a decent camera so you may snap pictures of the archeological site and its environs to save your memories of your trip to Pompeii.

5.2 Safety Advice

It is crucial to put safety first while visiting Pompeii to have a hassle-free and enjoyable experience. The following safety advice should be remembered:

1) **Keep on Designated routes:** to protect the historic ruins and to keep yourself safe, stay on designated routes and walkways while touring the archeological site.

2) **Take Care Where You Step:** Pompeii has rocky paths and cobblestone streets, making for an uneven landscape. Take care where you walk to prevent falling or sliding, particularly in places where there is loose gravel or debris.

3) **Keep Hydrated:** Especially on hot summer days, remain hydrated by drinking plenty of water during your visit. Keep a reusable water bottle with you, and stop often to relax and replenish your fluids.

4) **Observe Safety Signs and Rules:** Be mindful of the safety signs and rules that are placed all around Pompeii, particularly in sections that are being maintained or restored.

5) **Pickpocket Alert:** Although Pompeii is a generally secure place to visit, take care of your things and keep an eye out for pickpockets, particularly

in busy places or popular tourist destinations. When in busy areas, watch out for your belongings and use caution.

5.3 Pompeii's Dining and Shopping

After seeing Pompeii's archeological treasures, spend some time dining on the regional cuisine and perusing the local shops for mementos. Here are some suggestions for places to eat and shops in Pompeii:

1) **Local eateries:** Visit neighborhood trattorias and eateries to experience authentic Neapolitan food close to Pompeii. Savor traditional fare like pizza, spaghetti, and seafood as well as regional delicacies like limoncello (a lemon liqueur) and sfogliatella (pastry).

2) **Cafés and Gelaterias:** Stop by one of the Italian coffee shops or gelaterias close to Pompeii to indulge in gelato

and Italian coffee when you're not exploring. Enjoy cool granitas and creamy gelato varieties as you relax in the shade.

3) **Souvenir stores:** Look around for one-of-a-kind items and mementos to remember your trip to Pompeii in the souvenir stores and stands nearby. Look for locally produced goods that are inspired by Pompeii's rich history and culture, as well as handcrafted pottery and replica relics.

4) **Local Markets:** To purchase fresh fruit, cheeses, meats, and other delectable foods, visit the local markets in Pompeii and the surrounding towns. Mix with locals while taking in the lively ambiance of the marketplaces and tasting regional specialties.

While finding one-of-a-kind trinkets and mementos to bring home, travelers may fully immerse themselves in the local way of life and culinary traditions by exploring Pompeii's eating and shopping choices.

Chapter 6

Extending Past Pompeii

There are many archeological marvels to discover in Pompeii, but there are also plenty of other sites and day trip options nearby. This chapter provides ideas for day excursions from Pompeii and other sites to make the most of your vacation.

6.1 Day Excursions from Pompeii

Discovering more of Campania's rich cultural and historical legacy is possible by venturing outside of Pompeii. The following are some well-liked day excursion locations from Pompeii:

1) Tour Mount Vesuvius with a guide. Mount Vesuvius is the notorious volcano that destroyed Pompeii in 79 AD. Climb to the top for sweeping views of the Bay of Naples and

investigate the volcano's still-active crater.

2) **Herculaneum:** Take a tour of the adjacent Herculaneum archeological site (Ercolano), which is another old Roman city that was submerged in Mount Vesuvius' explosion. Herculaneum, a smaller and better-preserved site than Pompeii, provides insights into Roman everyday life.

3) Discover the dynamic city of Naples, which is renowned for its gastronomic pleasures, rich history, and cultural legacy. See the famous Piazza del Plebiscito, the Naples Archaeological Museum, and the Royal Palace of Naples, among other ancient sites.

4) Visit the quaint seaside town of Sorrento, which is well-known for its expansive vistas, attractive streets, and lemon trees. Explore the historic

center, take a stroll along the seaside promenade, and try the local specialty, limoncello.

5) **Amalfi Coast:** Enjoy a picturesque drive down the breathtaking Amalfi Coast, stopping to see quaint communities like Positano, Amalfi, and Ravello. Admire this UNESCO World Heritage Sites spectacular coastline cliffs, vibrant communities, and pristine waterways.

6) Explore the untamed coastline, posh shops, and natural wonders like the Blue Grotto and the Gardens of Augustus as you cruise to the opulent island of Capri. For amazing views, take the chairlift to the peak of Mount Solaro.

6.2 Convenient Nearby Sites

When visiting Pompeii, be sure to check out these neighboring sights in addition to day trip destinations:

1) The Pompeii Archaeological Museum is a neighboring city in Naples that is home to an extensive collection of antiquities, mosaics, and frescoes that have been unearthed from the ancient city of Pompeii. Additional perspectives on Pompeii's history and way of life may be gained from the museum.

2) Another well-preserved Roman villa buried by Mount Vesuvius is Villa Poppaea, which is located in the town of Torre Annunziata. Discover its gardens, opulent architecture, and paintings that portray episodes from mythology.

3) Visit the archeological site of Oplontis, which is said to be Poppaea Sabina, the second wife of Emperor Nero,'s suburban mansion. Admire the magnificent paintings and well-preserved buildings that provide

a sense of the opulence of ancient Rome.

4) **Vesuvian Villas:** Take a tour of the surrounding villas and ancient monuments, such as Villa Boscoreale, Villa Arianna, and Villa San Marco. These mansions, which include stunning murals and antiques, reflect the lavish lives of Pompeii's aristocracy.

5) **Wine Tasting Tours:** Take a guided wine-tasting trip to nearby vineyards and wineries to learn about the wine-producing area of Campania. Savor local wines like Lacryma Christi and take in the Amalfi Coast's and Vesuvius' vineyard scenery.

Travelers may explore further into the rich history, culture, and scenic beauty of the Campania area by venturing outside of Pompeii, which offers a variety of activities and sites to suit every interest.

Chapter 7

Conclusion

This chapter offers some advice and suggestions to make the most of your visit to the ancient city of Pompeii. It also gives you a chance to tell others about your experiences there.

7.1 Concluding Words of Wisdom and Advice

1) **Plan Ahead:** To make the most of your stay at the archeological site, learn about Pompeii's background, top attractions, and useful information before you arrive.

2) **Arrive Early:** Visit Pompeii in the morning when it's less crowded and the temperature is cooler to avoid the throng.

3) Refillable water bottles are a great way to keep hydrated when visiting, particularly on hot summer days.

4) **Wear Comfortable Shoes:** When touring the ruins of Pompeii, wear closed-toe shoes with adequate grip since the ground might be uneven.

5) **Respect the Site:** By being mindful of the ancient ruins, adhering to authorized walkways, and not touching or climbing on the monuments, you may help keep Pompeii intact for future generations.

6) **Take Breaks:** Throughout your stay, pace yourself and make time to relax, rehydrate, and take in Pompeii's atmosphere.

7) **Keep Memories:** To preserve your Pompeii experience, don't forget to take pictures and movies, but always

remember to show respect for both the site and other tourists.

7.2 Tell About Your Visit to Pompeii

We hope that your trip to Pompeii was enlightening and unforgettable! We want you to tell people about your experience at Pompeii, whether you enjoyed exploring the ancient ruins, were in awe of the exquisitely preserved objects, or discovered something new about ancient Roman life.

1) **Social media:** Use hashtags like #Pompeii, #AncientHistory, or #TravelMemories to share your best images and highlights from Pompeii on social media sites like Facebook, Instagram, and Twitter.

2) Contribute to travel forums and blogs by posting advice, suggestions, and first-hand stories about Pompeii to

assist other tourists in making travel plans to the archeological site.

3) **Reviews and Comments:** Share your thoughts on Pompeii in general and provide other visitors with insightful information by posting reviews and comments on travel websites, forums, and review platforms.

4) **Personal comments:** To ensure that your memories are preserved for years to come, take some time to think about your trip to Pompeii and record your ideas, observations, and comments in a notebook or travel diary.

You may educate and uplift others while remembering your tour through this remarkable archeological site by sharing your Pompeii experience with them.

We hope that after your trip to Pompeii, you will have a greater understanding of the city's ageless charm, rich cultural legacy, and ancient history. I hope you have a safe journey and that Pompeii will always be in your memory.

Printed in Great Britain
by Amazon

39812121R00030